BLANK VERSES

A PATHWAY TO EMOTIONS...

ABHINAV KESHARY

To my Mom,

To my Dad,

To my Dear ones

and Friends...

Contents

Foreword

His poetry pieces always provoke deep thought and are filled with emotion. They're consistently enjoyable to explore. -

Harshit Pal Singh, Author of Infinite Stanzas

A Good Friend

His poems are indeed with very deep meaning and have to lot to understand, very very good poems. -

A Good Friend

Abhinav, on his journey of world peace and spreading love, captures raw human emotions and unique insights into the human heart in each verse. His poems are truly inspiring, encouraging each one of us to become the best version of ourselves.-

Drishti, A Good Friend

His poems delve deep into intricate human emotion.-

Ritiesha Dahiya, A Good Friend

Preface

Welcome to Blank Verses, a collection crafted from the deepest recesses of the human experience. As you embark on this poetic journey, I invite you to approach these poems not merely as words on a page but as invitations to explore the very essence of your own emotions.

Every page contains a poem written with a deep emotion that one may feel it rather than just read it , I have written poems about tragedy, about loneliness ,about love , and about the current scenario of the world.

Each poem in this collection is a reflection of the complex and often intricate feelings that define our lives. I encourage you to read them with an open heart and a willing spirit. Let the verses resonate with you, and allow yourself to feel their rhythm and meaning deeply. This book is as much an exploration of your inner world as it is of mine. Embrace the emotions conveyed within these lines, and let them stir something profound within you.

Thank you for allowing Blank Verses into your life. I hope these poems speak

to you.

The *Blank Verses* is penned by the talented poet **Abhinav Keshary**. Abhinav's journey into the world of poetry has been one of profound introspection and heartfelt expression. Through his evocative verses, he captures the delicate emotions and fleeting moments that define our human experience.

Abhinav's work is a testament to the power of words to illuminate the soul and connect us to the deeper truths of our existence. "*Blank Verses*" is not just a collection of poems; it is an invitation to pause, reflect, and find beauty in the quiet moments of life. Each poem is a whisper that beckons us to listen more closely to the world around us and to the whispers within our own hearts.

• x •

Acknowledgements

I would like to extend my deepest gratitude to Notion Press Publishing for their invaluable support and dedication throughout the publishing process. Their expertise and commitment were instrumental in bringing this book to life.

A Big Thank You!

Prologue

BlankVerses explores the intricate tapestry of human emotions through evocative poetry. This collection delves into the depths of our inner lives, capturing the subtle and profound experiences that shape our existence.

Each verse is a reflection on the complexities of emotion, offering readers a window into the myriad feelings that define our shared humanity.

Through poignant and thought-provoking language, Blank Verses invites you to experience the beauty and turbulence of life's emotional landscape.

Quote

• xv •

دنیا کے لیے، آپ ایک شخص ہو سکتے ہیں، لیکن ایک شخص کے لیے آپ دنیا ہیں۔

To the world, you may be one person, but to one person you are the world
        -An Urdu quote

1. The Old Man

As I pass by the London bridge ,
I see this young old man .
A Happy young old man ,
Creased Oak hat.
And White hair,
For he, seems not to care.
A bowtie on his neck,
Gets the perfect serenity of wellness .
Carries a cigar,
Where it's smoke gets dispersed into city's air.
His pocket watch tucked on to his coat,
That has a lady's picture.
At the backdrop of darkness,
He gaises at the North star.
As the time passes by.

2. Boat

I row my own boat,
In the water full of piranhas.
That seek opportunity,
Opportunity to pull you down.
That lead to vast infinite ocean,
Where my boat doesn't seem to exist.
I see other ships,
From which I seek help.
But they must not,
Because they have travelled much.
From no boats to canoes and then to ships ,
For they, want everyone to go the same.
Struggle and Hard work are the lessons,
That one must learn.
One has to take the step,
Carve the steps and pave the step.
Thy one shall not look upon others success in glee,
But shall see their hardships.
One must not seek help,
One must stand on its own legs.
One must break the cage,
And then fly beyond.
I row my own boat,
I ought to row my boat.

3. The Great Banyan Tree

Shattered pieces of my heart ,
Hurt my feet .
As I walk over the loose string of hope ,
Loosened and by distrust .
Even when this is not sufficient ,
Then comes an arrow .
Arrows from their Jaws,
That pierce every part of my body .
The axe has already cut the stem ,
And the axemen are many ,
But then also;
Alone stands The Great Banyan Tree.

4. The Photograph

One will pass another will go,
But the picture won't .
It's a simple piece of cardboard ,
That owes a lot .
From tables to shelves ,
Places may change .
But it's place in-
Our hearts would never change .
They are the become a collection
-Of priceless memory ,
That every man leaves behind.
The body and the soul are gone ,
But still they can revive their presence .
These pictures might get old ,
But the happy faces would never...

5. Venom

Today it's everywhere,
Not in a bowl or a cup.
But present in one's mind,
Present on the tongues.
They do not speak ,
But shoot arrows of Envy.
We are living on the land of snakes,
Where everyone hisses.
Only a few are venomous.
Thou' this venom shall not pierce,
Pierce your Pride.
One needs to be immune,
Immune from this venom.
One shall not be affected,
Or might get constricted.
Like a Rabbit in Python's trap,
Which then suffoctes and loses its presence,
Presence from this venomous world.

6. The Reason

Land will remain ,
While the lives would be slain .
Water would be there ,
The nature doesn't seen to care .
What will erode
- Is Humanity ,
Kingdoms would turn into a bloody sea .
History will witness all ,
That nobody cares at all .
These petty games are played ,
By the Demons of Money , Greed and Power in shade .
Or it doesn't even matter ,
Particles of dust appears like the latter.

7. The Great Indian Monsoon

Black clouds skuddle in the clear sky,
Cool wind starts to blow.
Avians rush around,
The raven caws
Hawks and eagles come around ,
Soaring high up in the sky.
Few strings of sunlight,
Appear from the corner in the sky,
First big drops hit the severed earth.
Water starts flowing,
Filling up the pathways.
Drop by drop,
The water sums up.
Wiping everything on it's way,
Bashing and dashing here and there
Banging into the concrete jungle,
As it makes its way.
Washing plants, washing trunks,
-washing away; the fragile little lives,
This is The Great Indian Monsoon.

8. Sunk and Sunk

Clouds coming by,
As the air is still.
Thunderstruck waters roaring nearby,
I was dragged along.
To accept the fate,
Where I was headed.
Water is filling up,
But I won't do a thing.
My torso sunk and sunk and sunk
till my nose,
I breathe in the serendipity of calm environment.
I sink and elevate,
Elevate above the clouds.
Seeing my lifeless body immersed
In the ocean floor.

9. By the clouds.

I came by the clouds,
Watched a lot of chaos.
I came to the ground,
- and saw shattered pieces of Humanity.
I came to their mind,
They were stressed , pleading to leave -
Leave all those sins,
Leave all those memories ,
Leave this body .
I came to their hearts ,
I saw them cry .
Then I met their souls,
- and felt so depressed that .
What's the point of moulding them?

10. Forgiveness

I seek forgiveness from mother Earth ,
What may a single homage is do ?
She cries day and night .
Innocent souls depart every night,
Who shall she complain to ?
She has been soaked up in blood and cry,
As her children die .
I am a poet ,I must say ,
I always pray .
But people will leave ,
Leave they sayings away .
Question the people in grey ,
Till when shall it stop?

11. I Live in a World Where...

I I live in a world,
Where politics is a key to delopment.
I live in a world,
Where people live and die, nobody cares.
I live in a world,
Where people support and take side, even if
- it's a war zone.
I live is a world,
Where anything's taken for granted.
I live in a world
Where people fight over GOD and LAND.
I live in a world,
Where demons of money, greed and power,
have come out of HELL!

12. Definition of War

Definition of War,
Surely the inner demons will roar.
It's just not a fight between Kingdoms,
Neither playing warcries resonating with drums.
It's like an unplanned calamity,
These games are seriously petty.
It's like enriching the earth with blood,
This planet would know the history of the RED BLOOD.
It's criminals enjoy the cake,
While put the innocent lives at stake.
They will get this fruits afterlife.
So one can judge their life.
War is more than arms,
Where one loses one's charm.
Wars is more than supporting teams in a game,
Because teams are cheered in a game not in a war, that came.
This is Definition of War,
Surely the inner demons will roar.

13. Love of a Man.

Love is not defined by genders ,
But it's genderless .
Love does not have definition,
Or any boundaries .
Human love is the most important love ,
That one must learn .
Killing others doesn't make you lovable ,
But rather locks you and your soul inside the cages of Brutality .
I am a poet, I must may fight with my pen ,
With my words as I say .
But it depends upon you ,
Whether you prioritise human love
- Or support sides in this massacre.

14. Love is Love

Love is Love
Love has no age
Love has no body
It's the souls that get entwined
True strings of Hope and Faith
Two parrots in the sky
In the backdrop of infinite stars
Fly together
As the Sun never sets
Trancends to the true meaning
Of real Love

15. Isolation

When I come here,
Then it feels so little in here.
Life just waits for another ,
Everything's on the third gear.
Happy ,Sad ,Crying, and Fun faces,
My heart is tied in laces.
Even when I fly ,I can't collect clouds,
I just not depends ; upon the crowds.
Thy yourself is best, that you can really emphasize ,
That I suffice.
It's not okay but better,
To give you yourself to cater.
Let you be happy with you,
Shouldn't we change to what others do!

16. Energies within us (Divided)

I was working by the dark alley,
Devil came and asked.
Why thou' shall I not exist?
Even if god is there.
Why not me ?
There is no god no devil !
It's the universe .
There's no greed for Devil nor God for power,
These are just different energies .
That one must balance ,
In order to attain Harmony .
Then the Devil cried and vanished,
In the backdrop of rising Sun .
I asked myself ,
What's the difference between God and Devil ?
When both live in heavenly bodies ,
And have powers more than that of a man.

17. Break it.

The sweat drops,
Travelling from forehead to side cheek.
Drop by drop ,
On the shuddering body .
The body respires heavily ,
As if any fish is starving without water.
One bites nails ,
Indicating all .
The feeble body ,
Even gets more feeble.
Brain starts to get unstable ,
Adrenaline pours down .
Break it.
For he , isn't dying ,
Everything would remain the same .
The earth , the rocks,
The same you .
Important is not winning or losing ,
But the knowledge that one acquires .
Going through the pressure ,
One gets to know more.

18. Pens of Poets

Poet have pens,
Pens to fight .
Where no one is killed ,
Where no one is harmed .
We have sword like pens,
Which till the hideous skin of society.
We have arrows like pens ,
Which shoots arrows .
Right into its eye ,
We have paper .
That resembles this society ,
Stories can be manipulated
- but the Poems can't.

19. God.

Every soul on this soil
Is the child of the God
Every soul rushes to get into this melancholy
Only the God knows why
Every soul wants to earn paper
But any process
They forget
- Forget that they are still the children of the God
When the soul struggle to find
Bread and wine
The God offers his child
When the soul strangles itself
The God unstrangles it
The God is supreme
Thou' shall not forget the past

20. End of Monstrous Life.

We are Humans,
- rather live a fragile life.
We can live,
Live without GUNS and WARS,
Live without DEMARKATIONS and BORDERS,
Live without MONEY and POWER,
But what have they done to us.
We were supposed to be an intelligent race,
We are stuck and addicted to this maze.
WITH Every man, Every child who would be
-dying in this unknown war!
One may say this, these lines may be forgotten,
But it's enough to create impact,
An impact to save Humanity,
Humanity that we have had lost long ago.
We have to fight,
Fight mentally,
-to End of monstrous Life!

Epilogue

Thank you for coming with me throughout this poetic journey of mine, I would continue to write more.

Though, it's just the starting I personally felt very happy and very satisfied after expressing my deep emotions for very intricate moments of human life, through my poem, through my book.

Thank you for bringing Blank Verses your life.

This means a lot to me.